How To Draw Castles And Build Imaginary Kingdoms

Drawing a Castle from Start to End: Detailed Steps

How to Draw Castles

By : Gala Publication

2

Published By :

Gala Publication
© Copyright 2015 – Gala Publication

ISBN-13: **978-1522800958**
ISBN-10: **1522800956**

Table of Contents

KIDS CASTLE

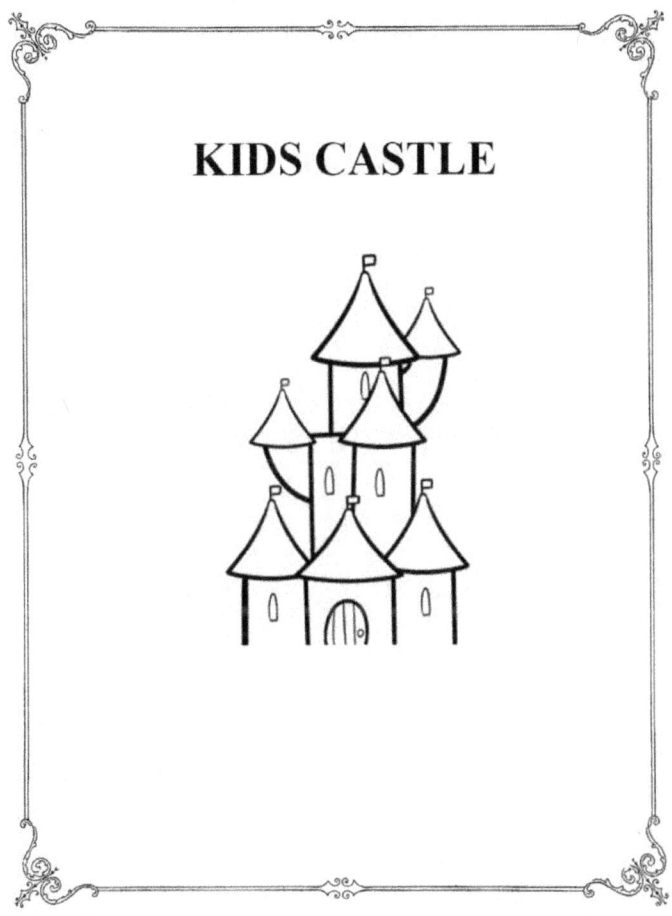

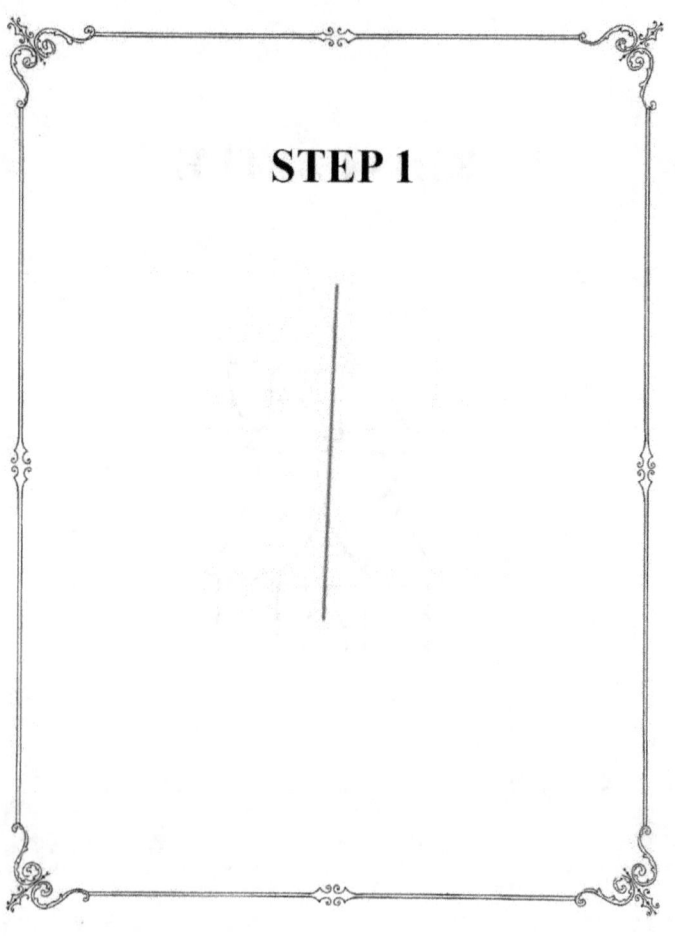

STEP 1

STEP 2

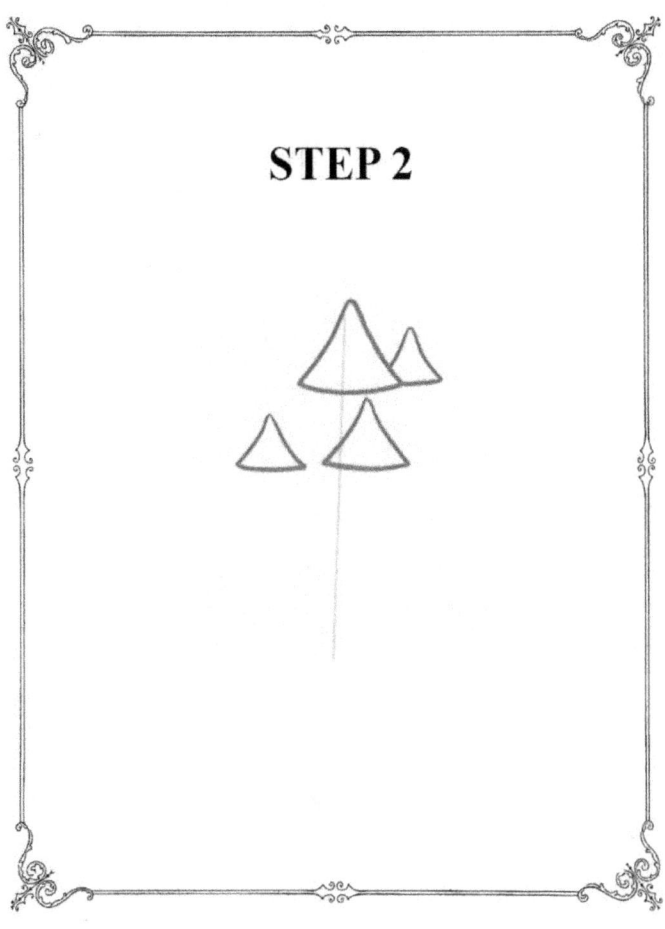

STEP 3

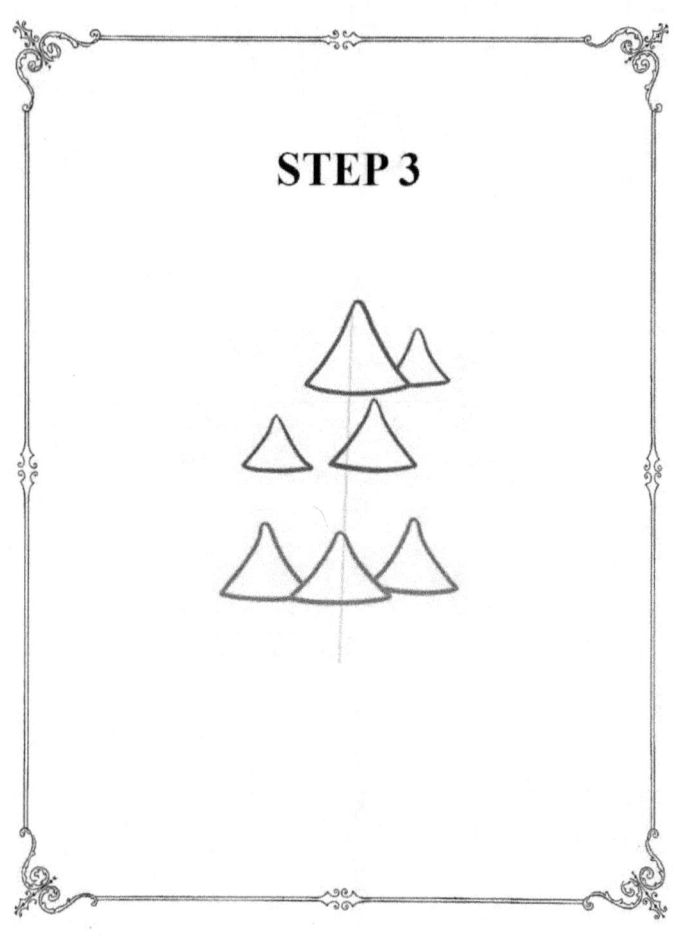

STEP 4

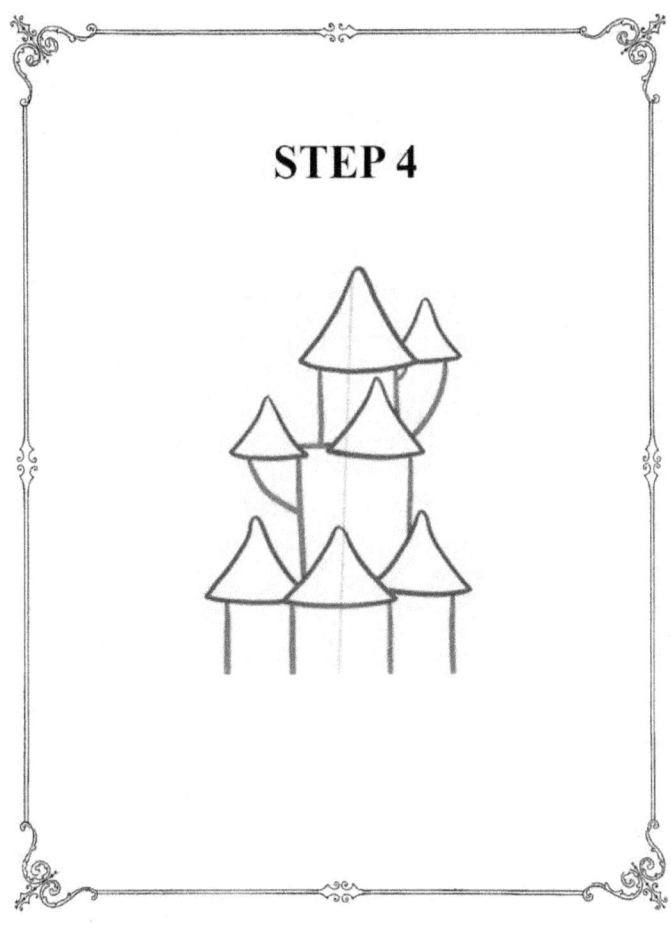

STEP 5

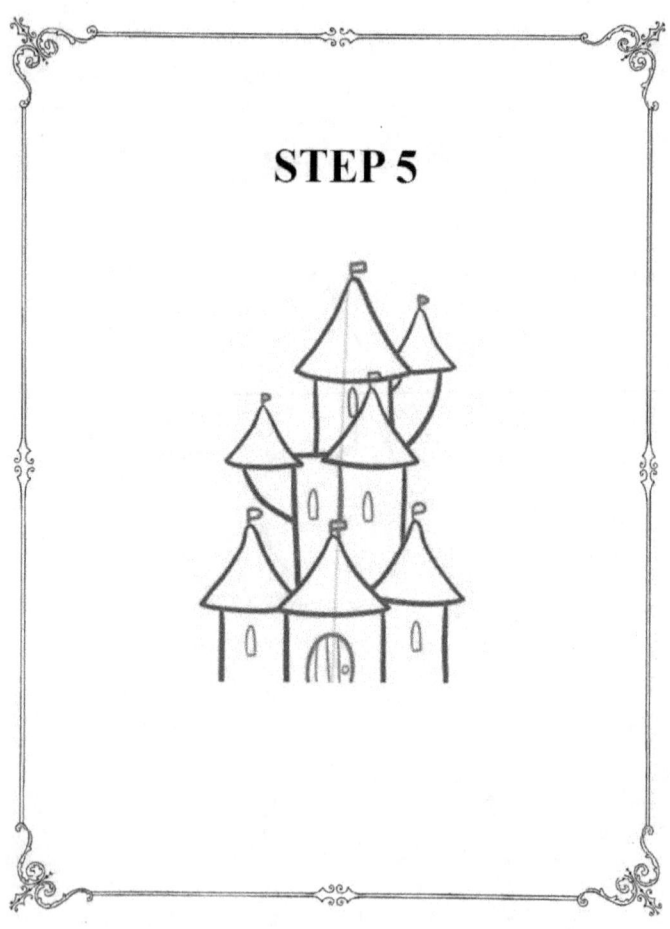

STEP 6

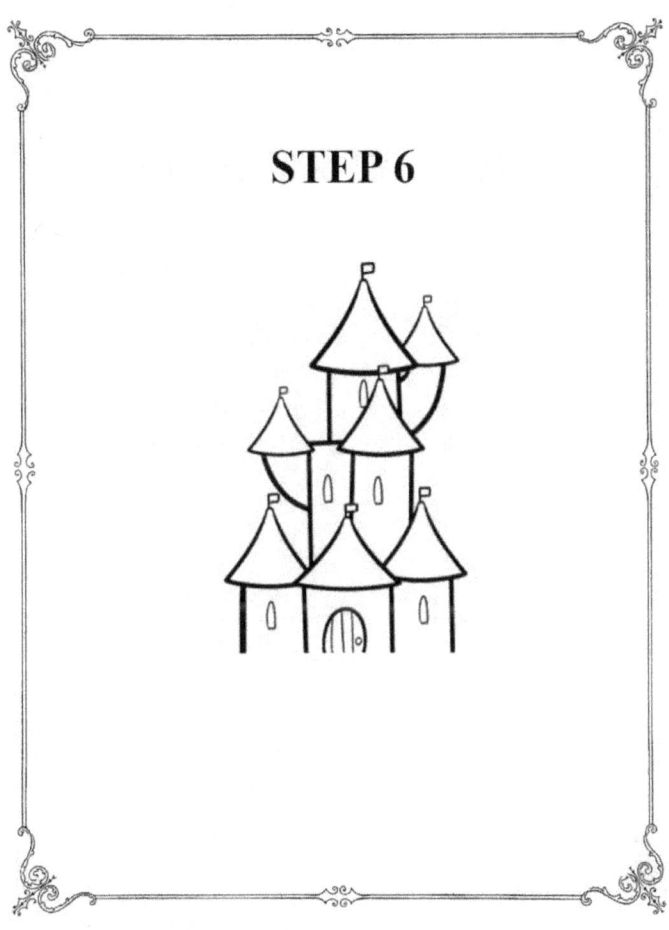

PRINCESS CASTLE

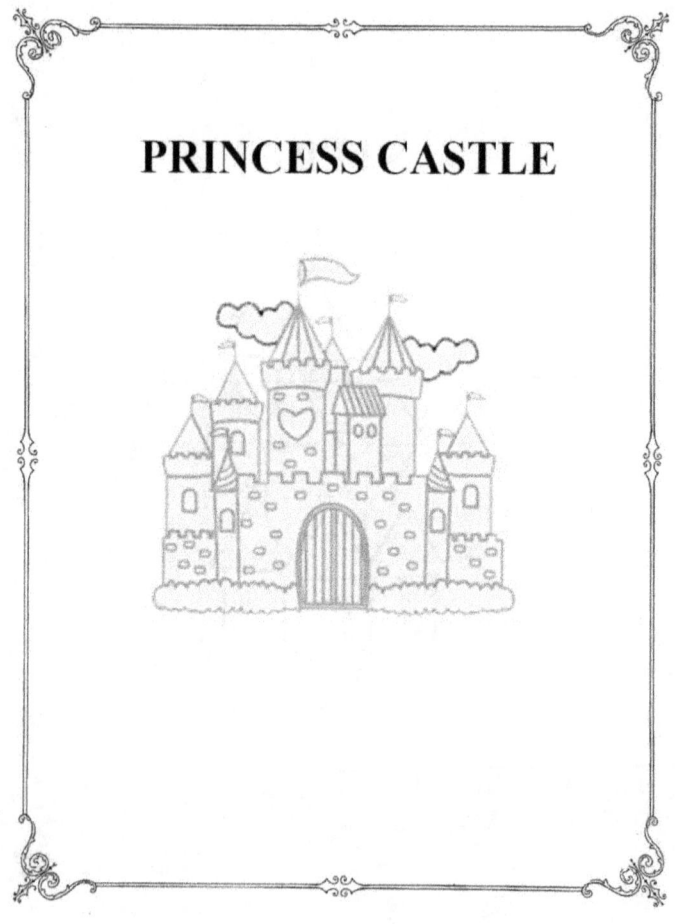

STEP 1

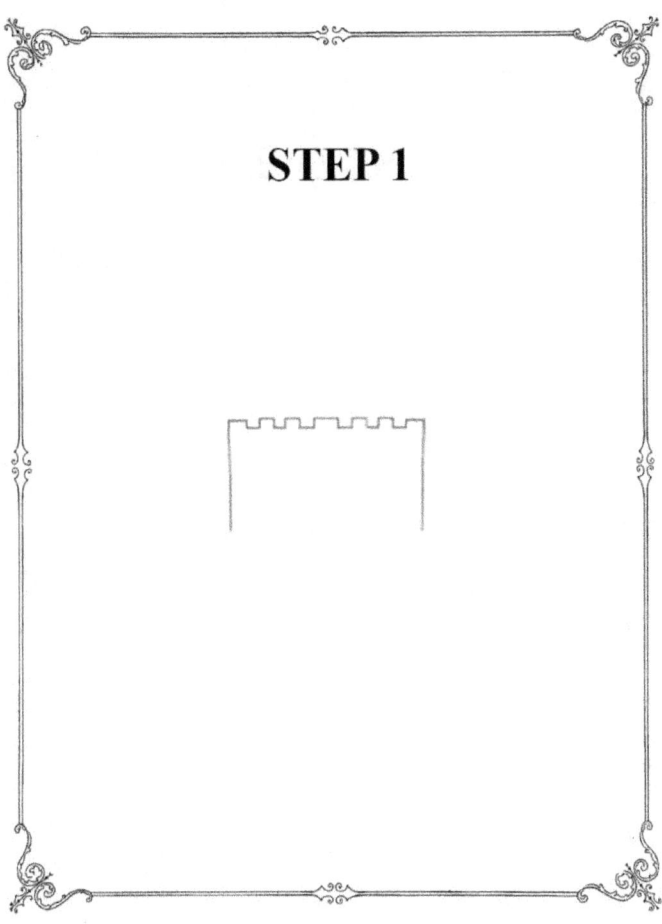

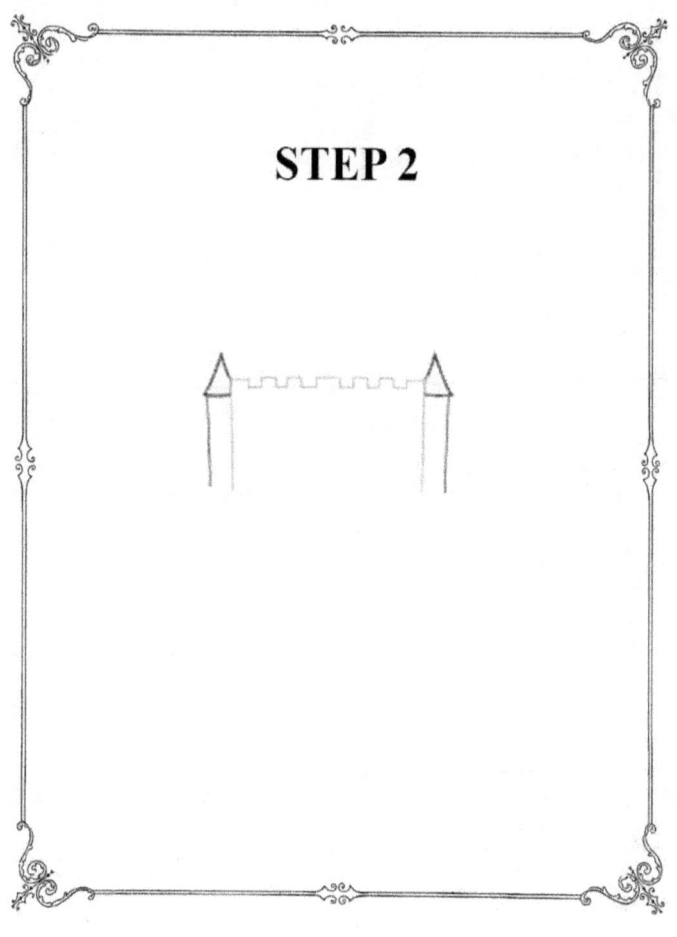

STEP 3

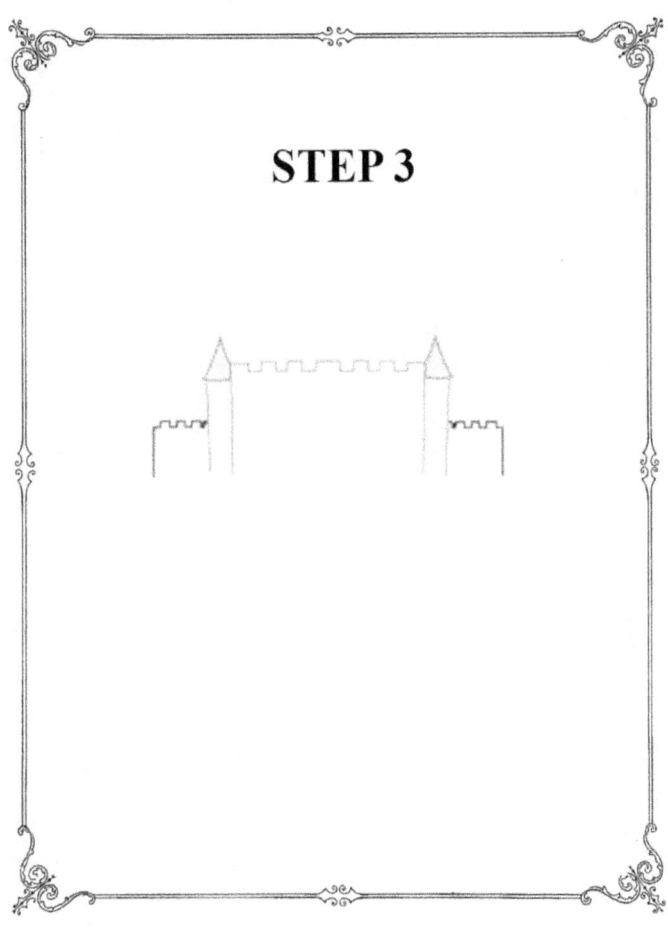

STEP 4

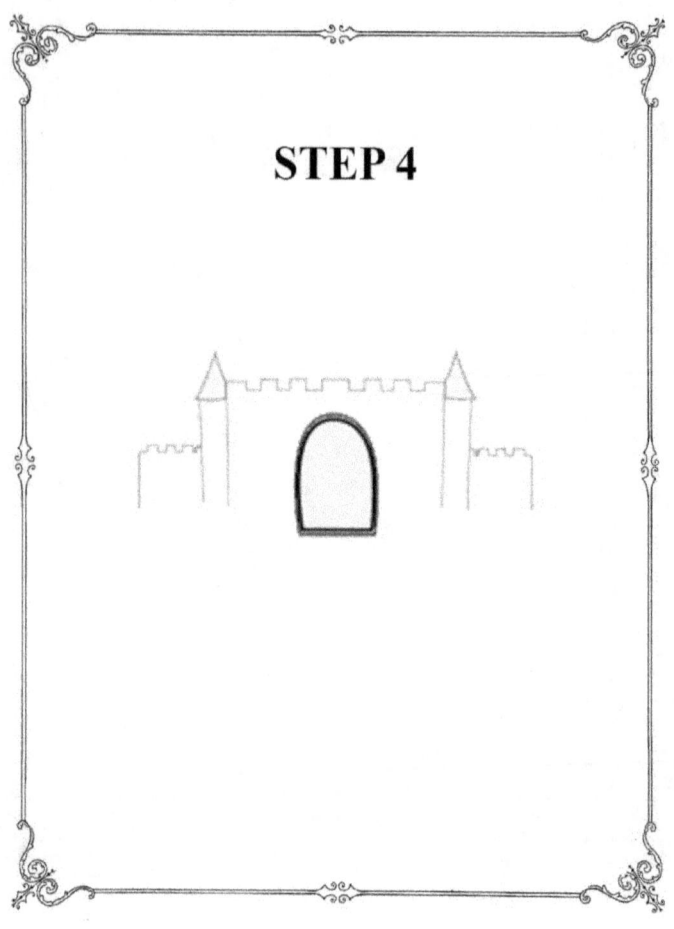

STEP 5

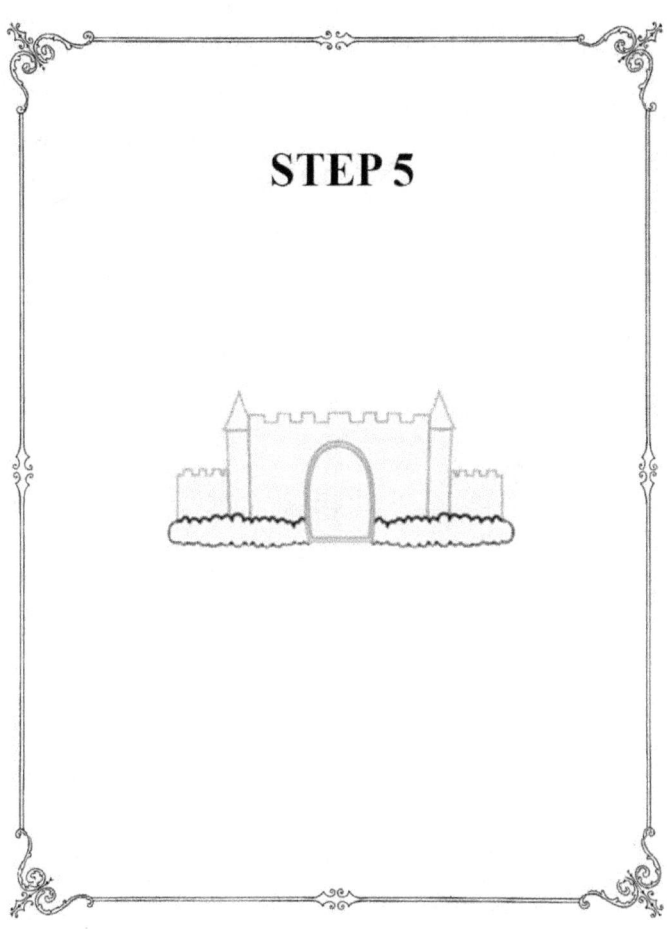

STEP 6

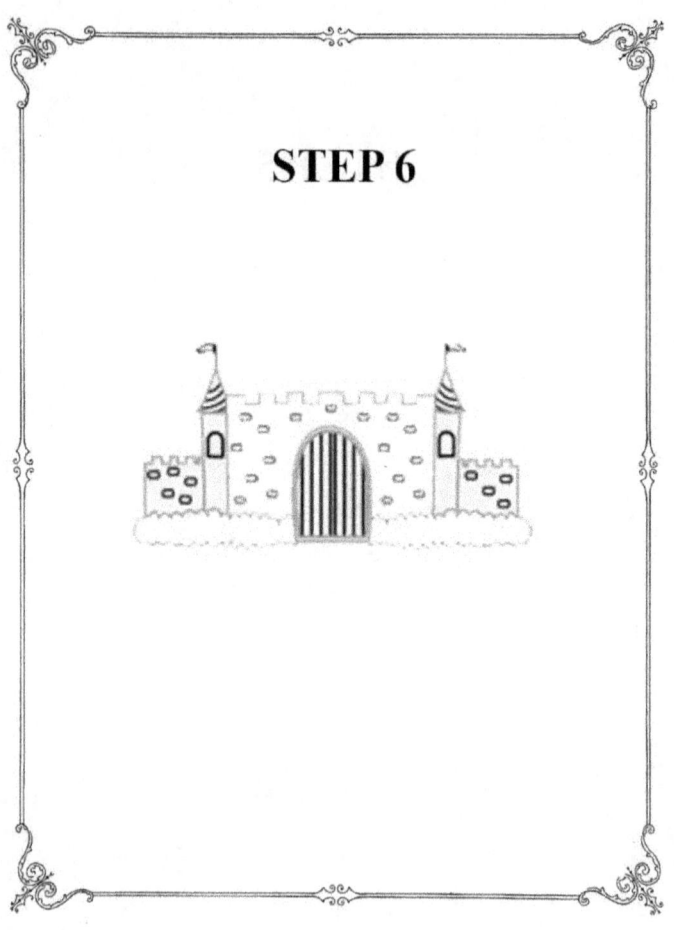

STEP 7

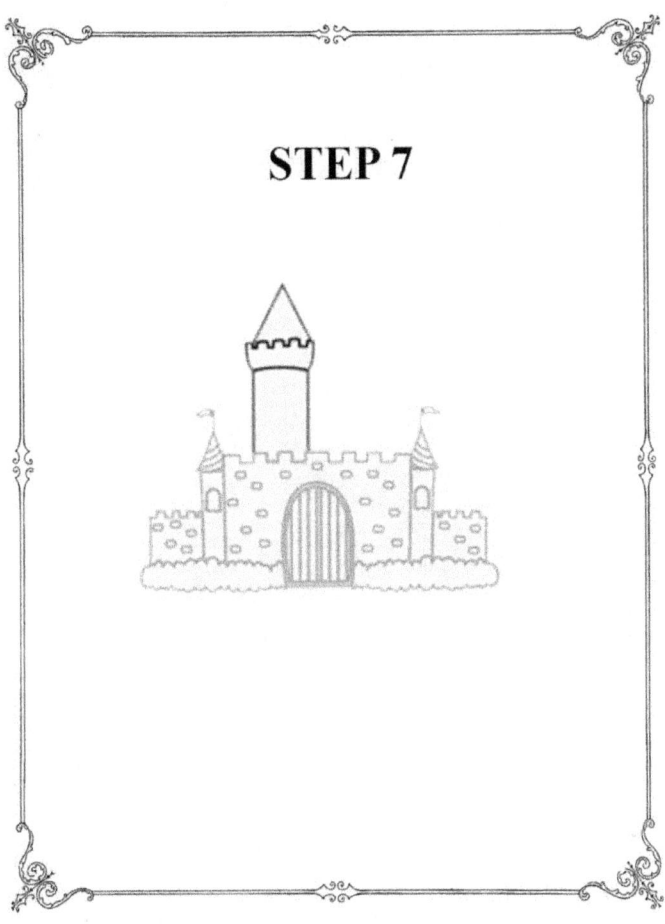

STEP 8

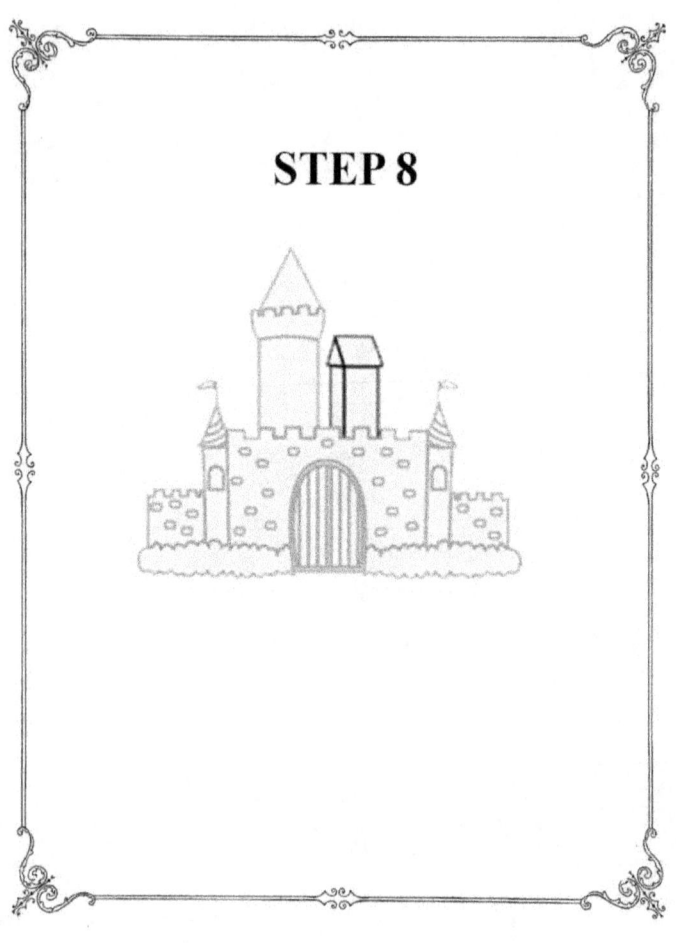

STEP 9

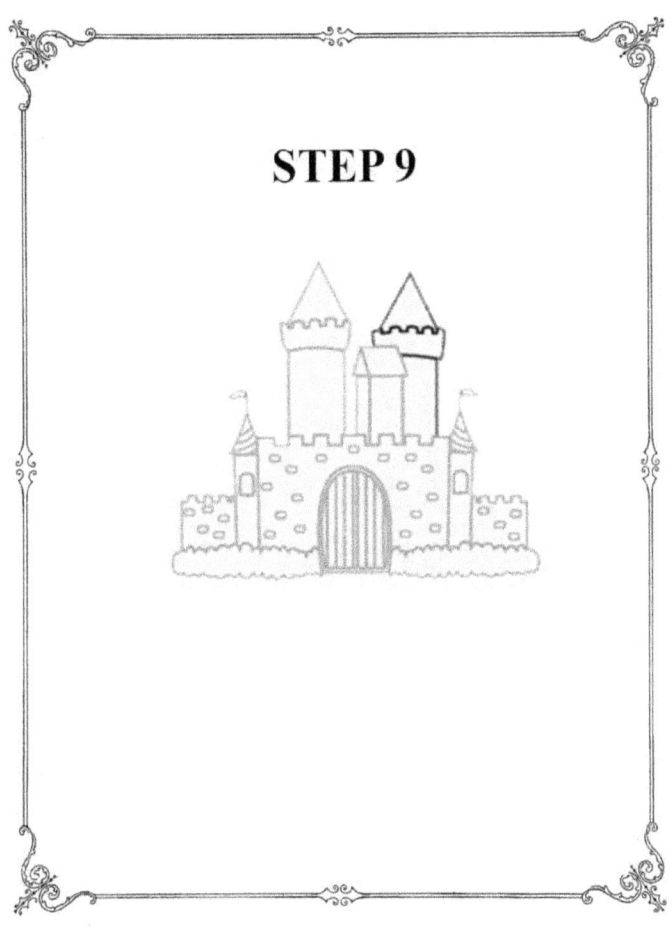

STEP 10

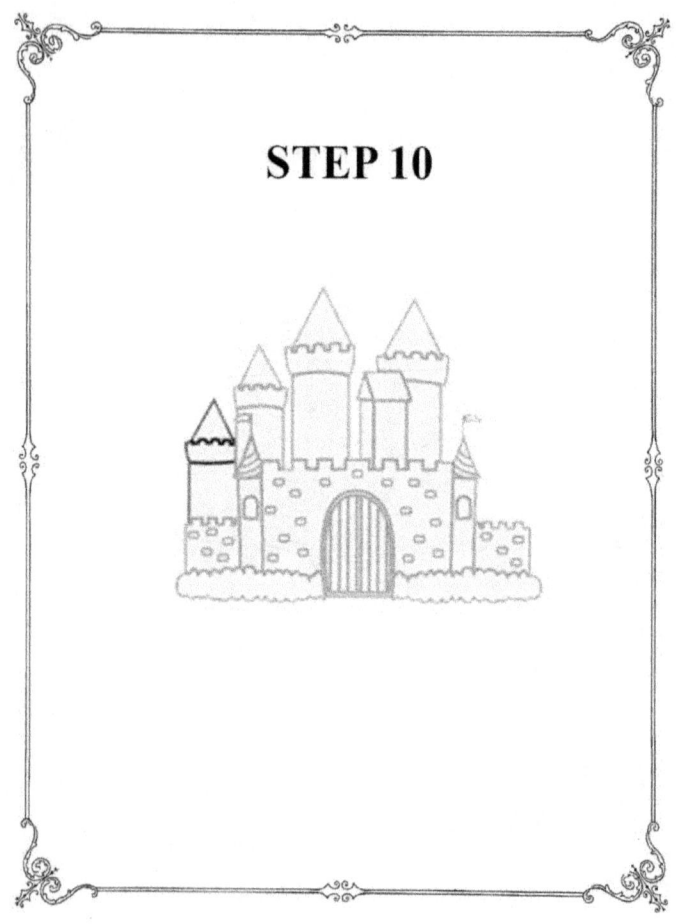

STEP 11

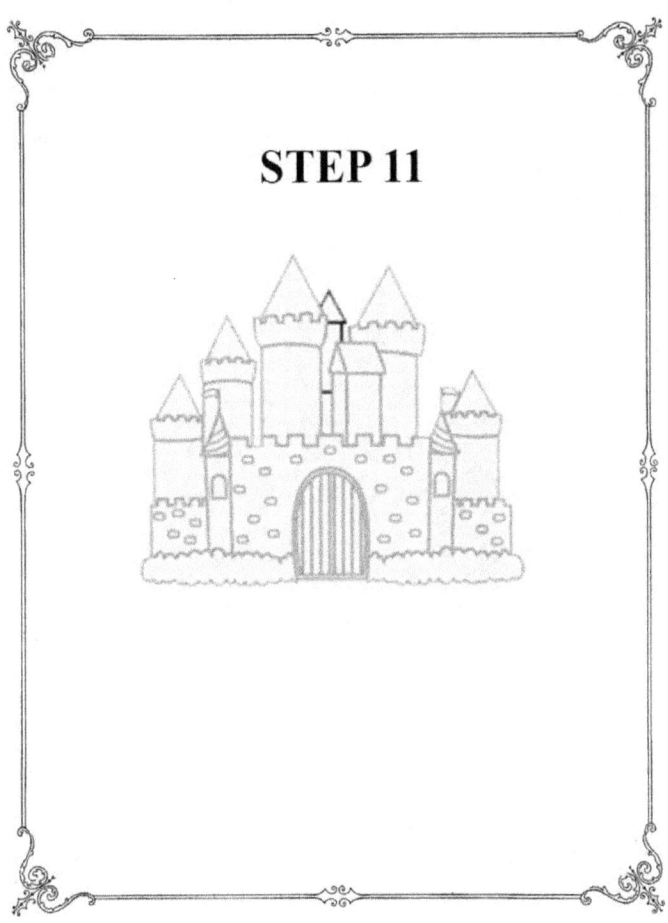

STEP 12

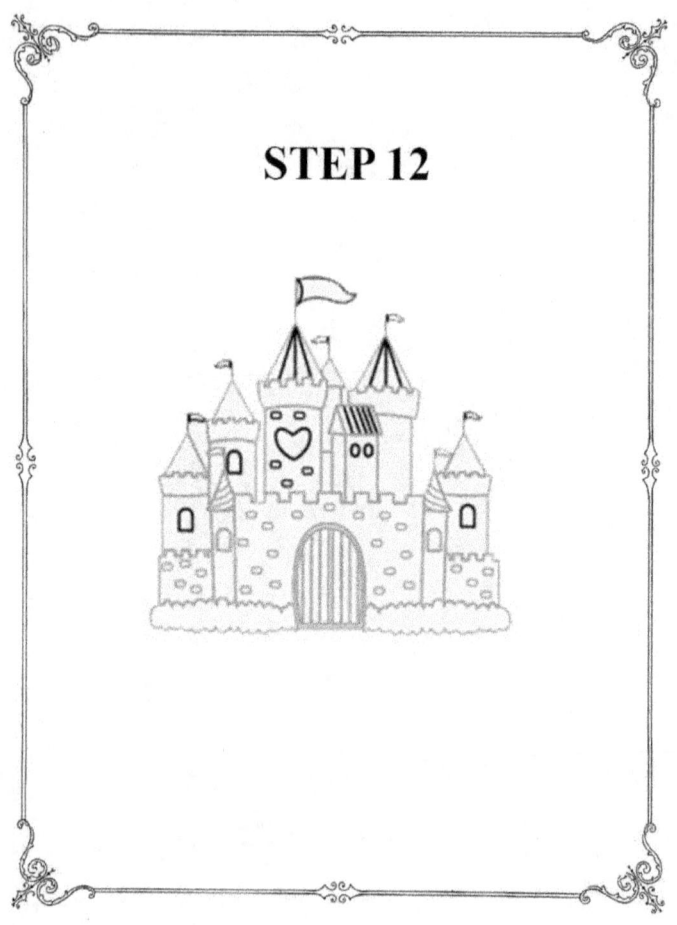

STEP 13

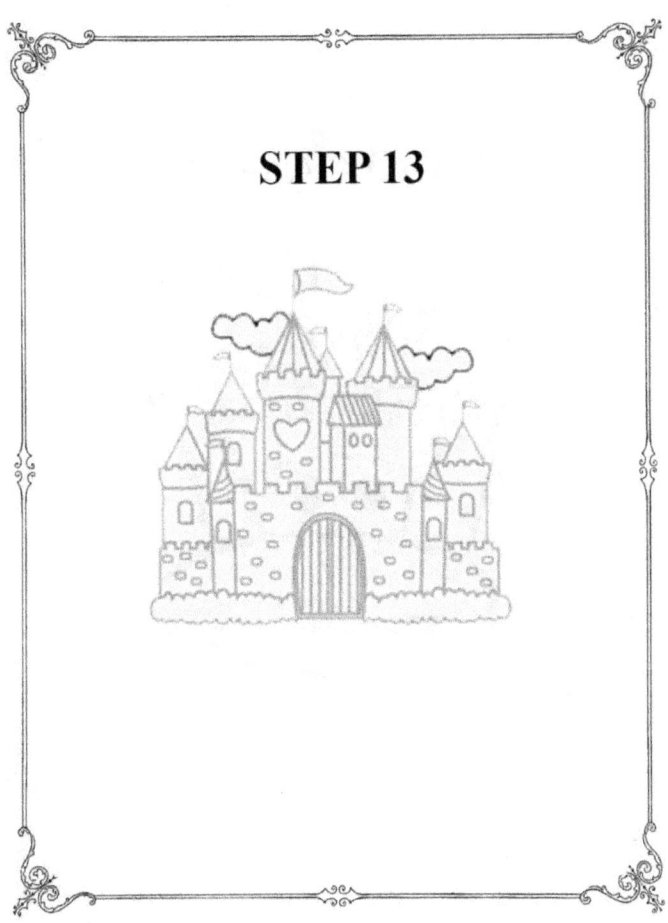

SAND CASTLE

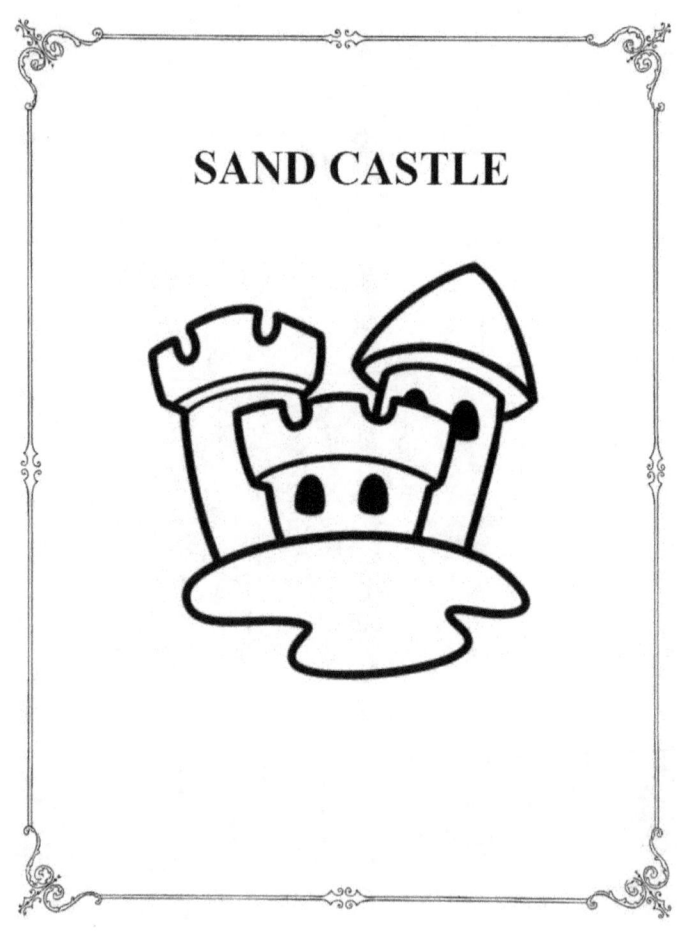

STEP 1

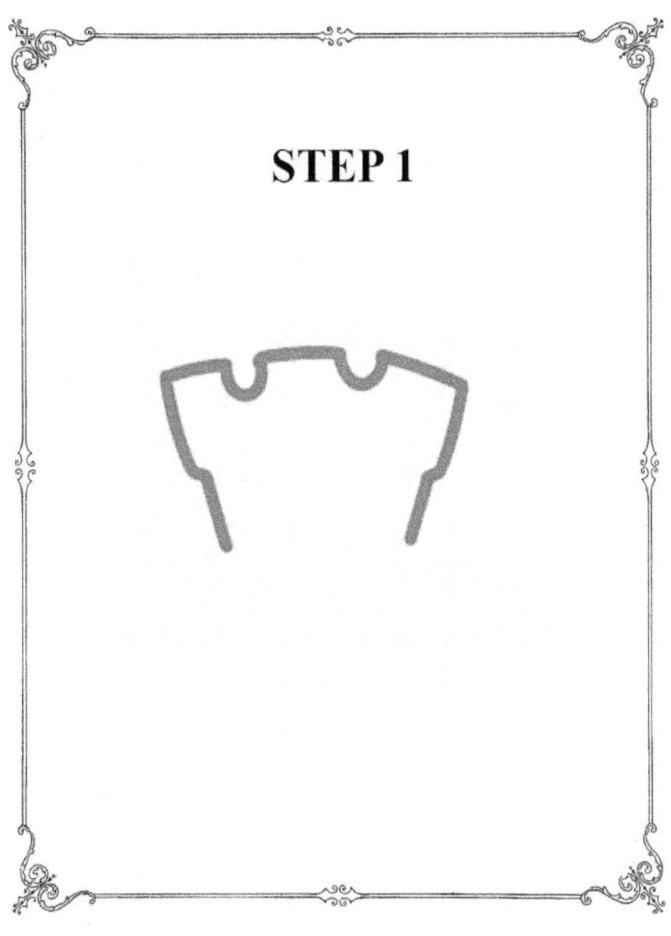

STEP 2

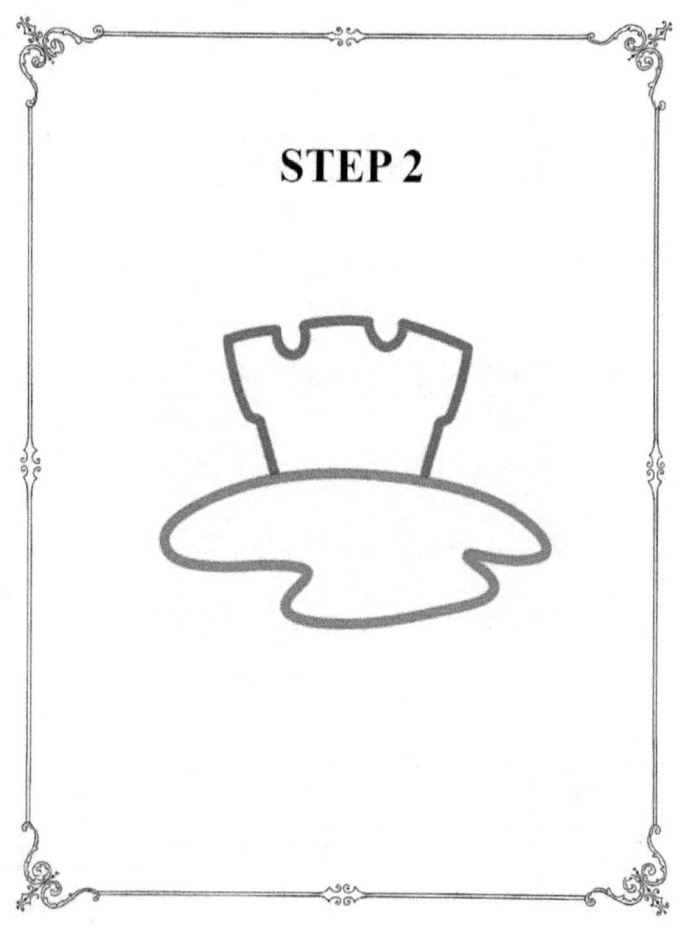

STEP 3

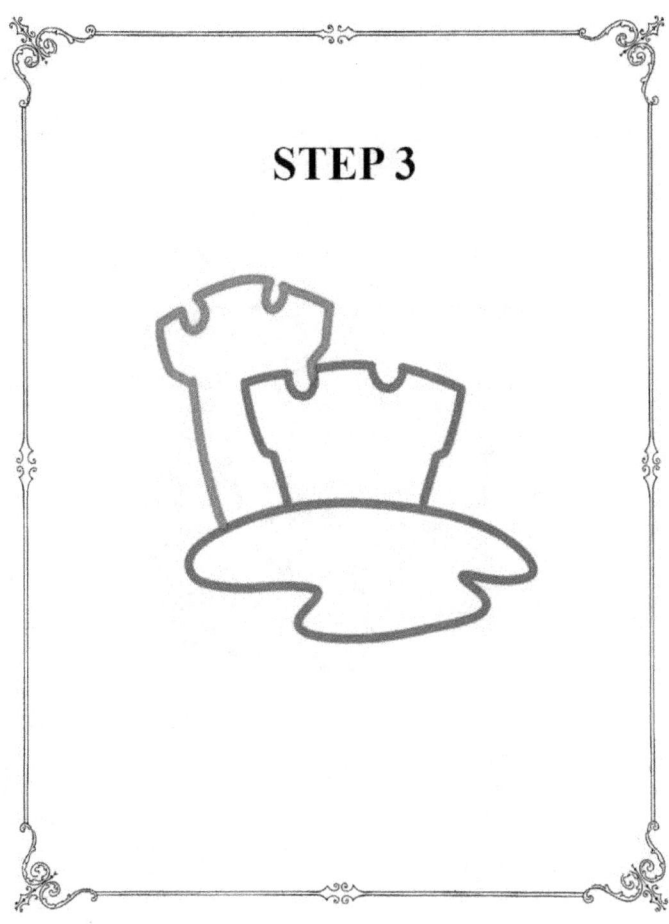

STEP 4

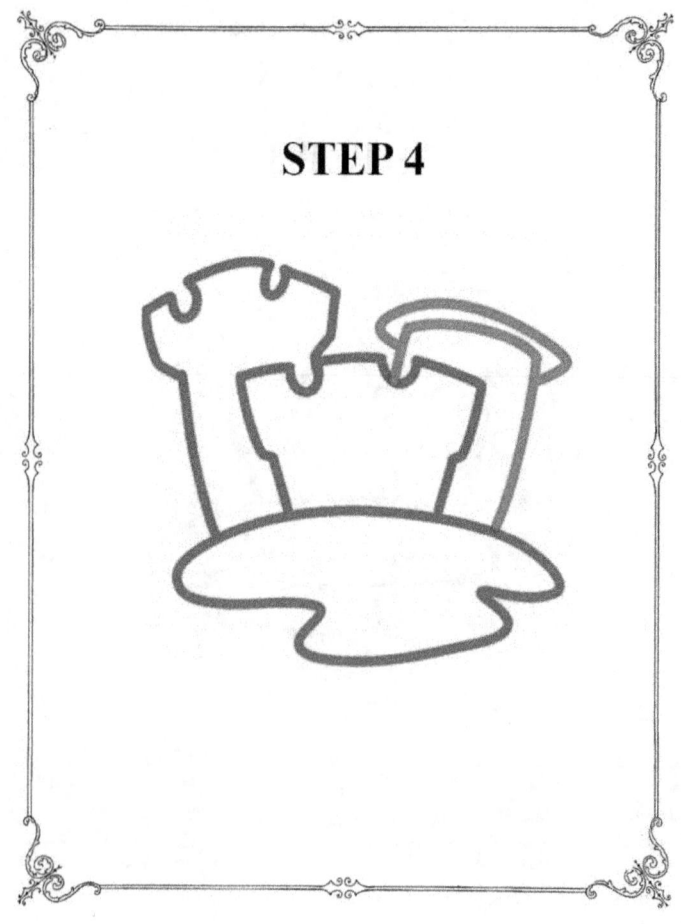

STEP 5

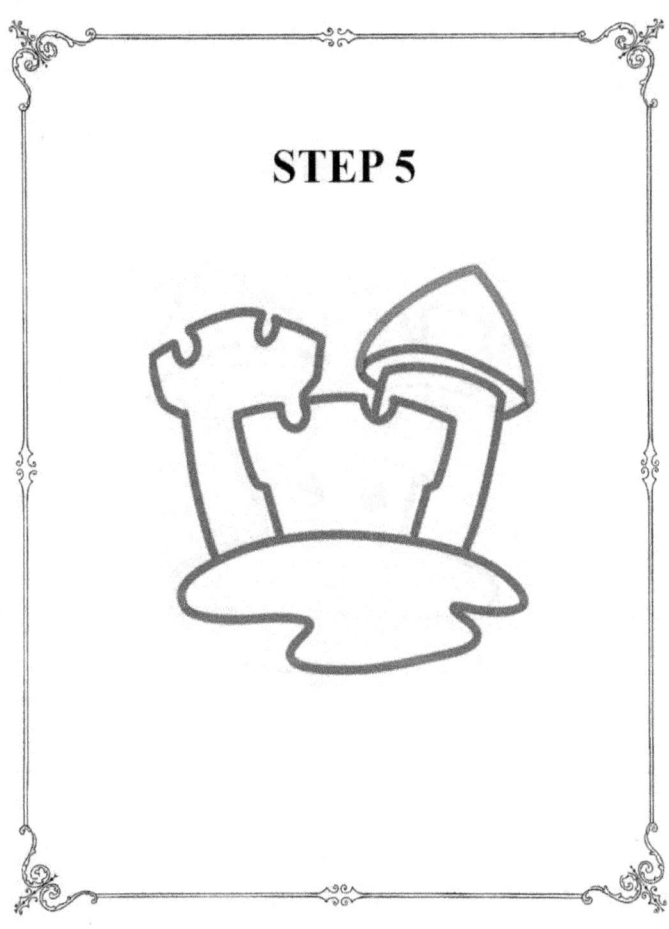

STEP 6

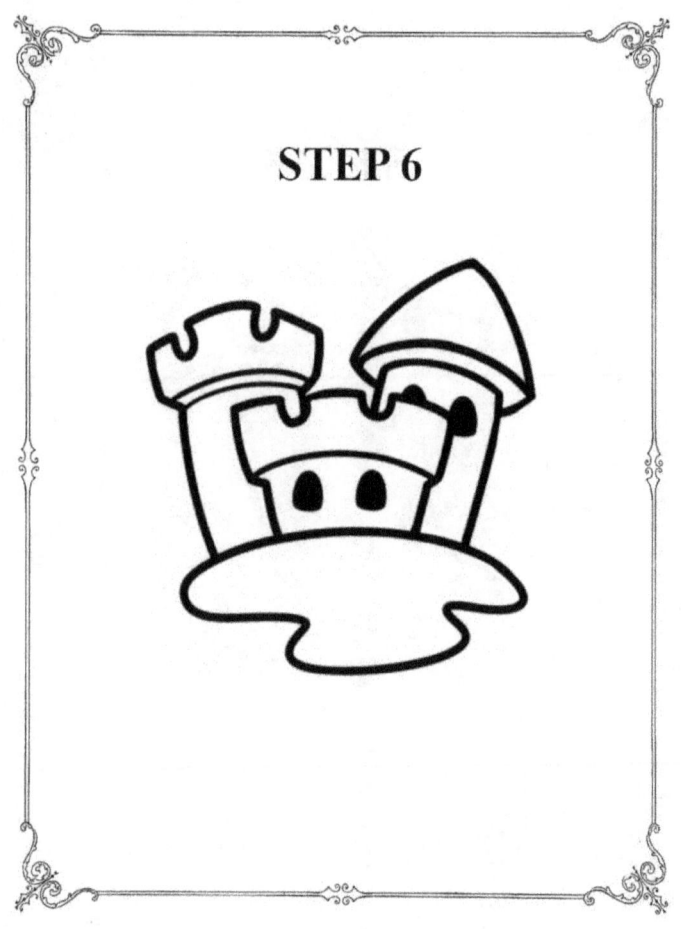

33

SIMPLE CASTLE

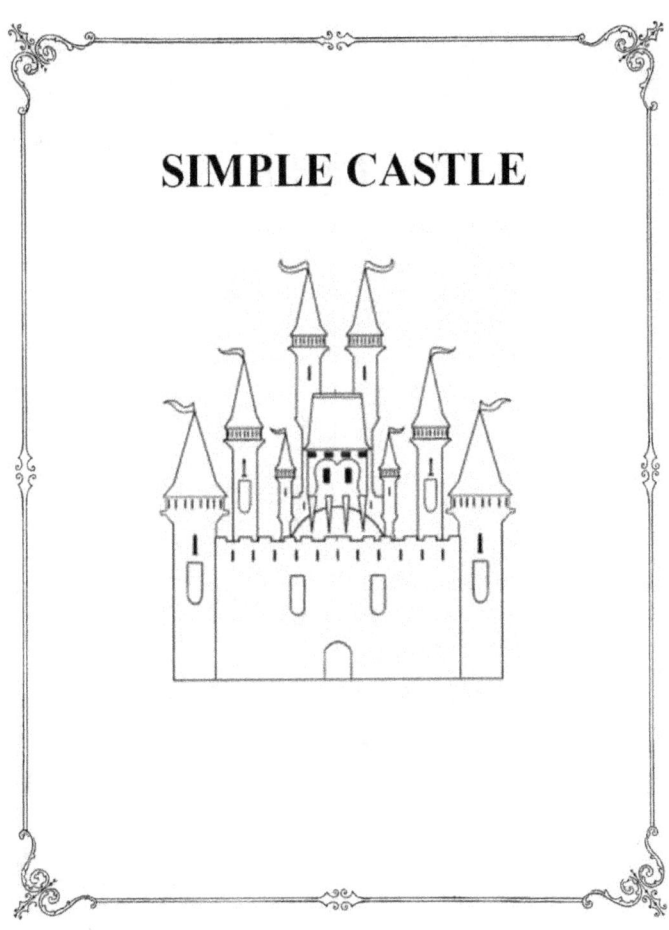

STEP 1

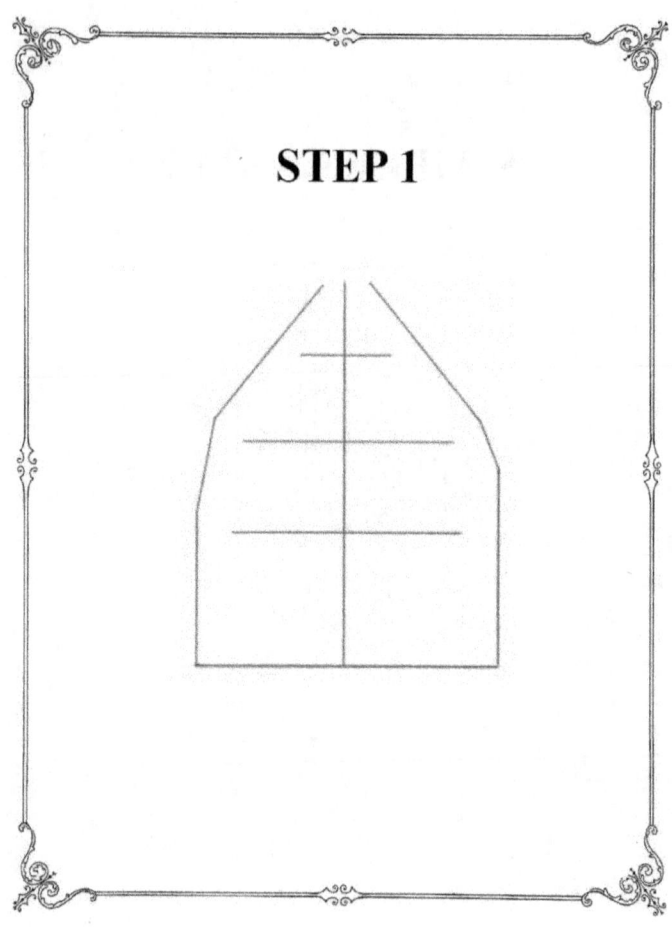

STEP 2

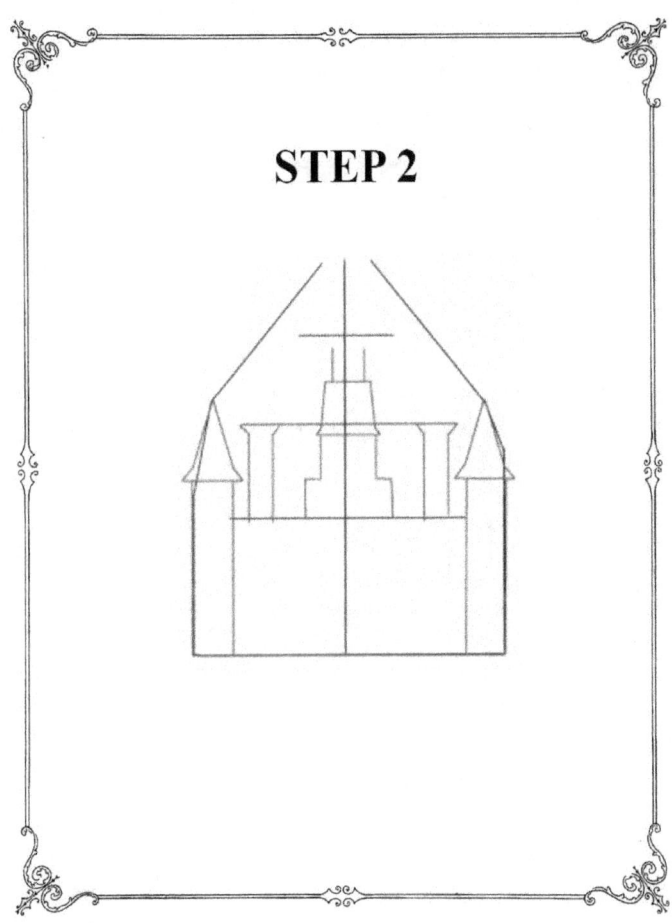

STEP 3

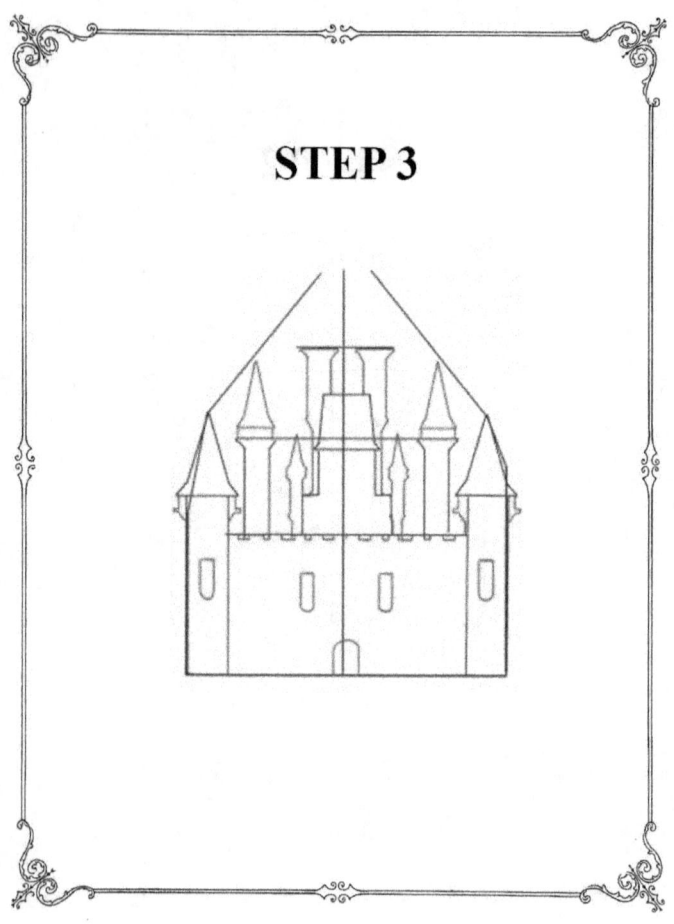

STEP 4

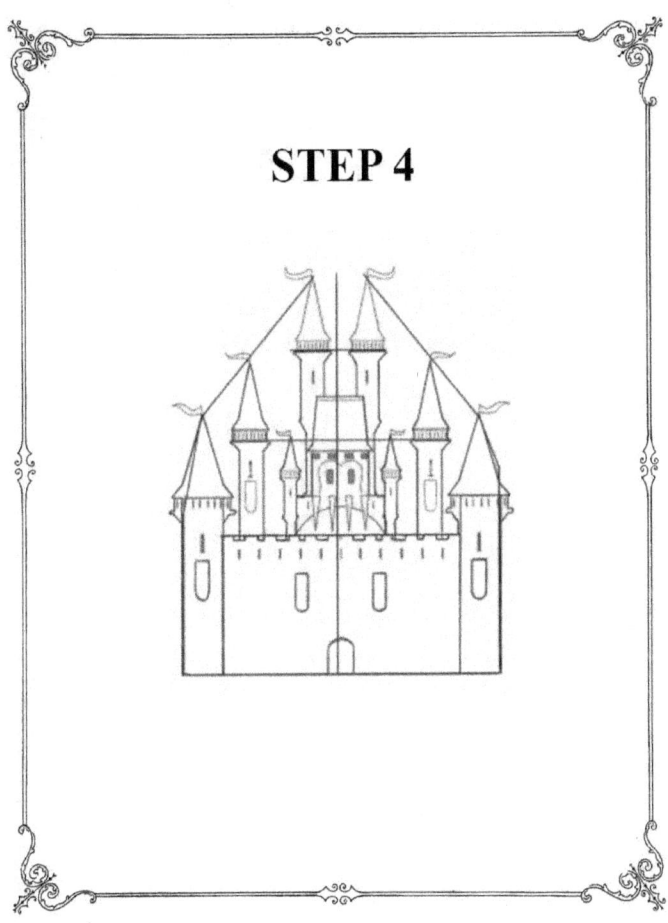

STEP 5

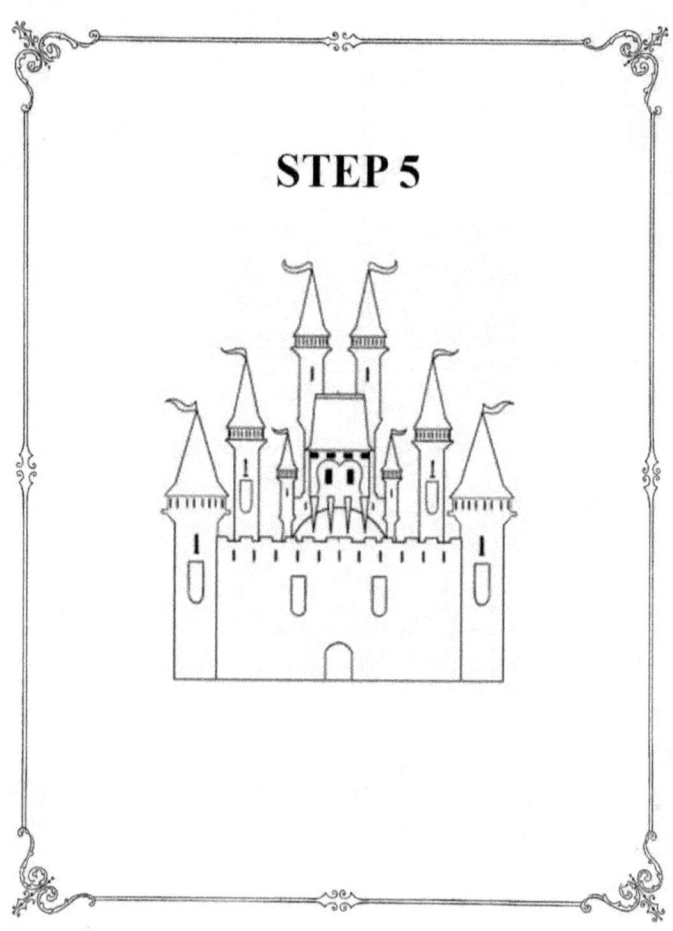

www.ingramcontent.com/pod-product-compliance
Lightning Source LLC
Chambersburg PA
CBHW071550170526
45166CB00004B/1621

* 9 7 8 1 5 2 2 8 0 0 9 5 8 *